DON'T SEND A

RESUME

ALSO BY JEFFREY J. FOX

How to Become a Rainmaker

How to Become CEO

DON'T SEND A

RESUME

And Other
Contrarian
Rules to Help
Land
a Great Job

JEFFREY J. FOX

New York

Library of Congress Cataloging-in-Publication Data

Fox, Jeffrey J., 1945–
Don't send a resume: and other contrarian rules to help land a great job /
Jeffrey J. Fox.
p. cm.
ISBN: 0-7868-6596-2
I. Job hunting. I. Title.

HF5382.7 .F68 2001
650.14—dc21
00-066368

FIRST EDITION

10   9   8   7   6   5   4   3   2   1

ACKNOWLEDGMENTS

Mary Ellen O'Neill, Hyperion senior editor. Stern, but never cross, with deadline-dodging, deadbeat authors (so I've heard).

Doris S. Michaels, head of the eponymously named New York City literary agency that deals with stern but never cross senior editors.

Consigliere. The only person who said, "Go for it." (See Chapter XLIV.)

Jerry Sindell, Tiburon, California. If you have a book in you, he can get it out.

CONTENTS

Introduction   1

• I •

Don't Send a Resume   5

• II •

Why Resumes Don't Sell   8

• III •

The Job-getting Blueprint   12

• IV •

Skip the Personnel Department   14

• V •

The Job Seeker's Marketing Mix   18

{ix}

CONTENTS

· VI ·

The Job Seeker's Glossary   22

· VII ·

You Are a Box of Cereal   25

· VIII ·

Always Dollarize Yourself   28

· IX ·

Draw a Forty-mile Circle   33

· X ·

How to Research a Target Company   36

· XI ·

Look Where They Ain't   41

· XII ·

Write an Impact Letter   47

· XIII ·

Write Boomerang Letters   54

CONTENTS

· **XIV** ·

Send a Resu-letter   60

· **XV** ·

Be a Fish out of Water   64

· **XVI** ·

Don't Play Resume Roulette   67

· **XVII** ·

Nontraditional Clues for Writing a Resume   71

· **XVIII** ·

No One Cares about Your Job Objective   77

· **XIX** ·

Don't Play *What's My Line?*   81

· **XX** ·

The Job Interview Is a Sales Call   85

· **XXI** ·

Answer the Question, Why Should This
Company Hire Me?   89

CONTENTS

• **XXII** •

Always Have a Sales Call/Job Interview
Objective   92

• **XXIII** •

Precall Plan Every Job Interview   95

• **XXIV** •

Job Interview Precall Planner   99

• **XXV** •

No One Cares What You Like   105

• **XXVI** •

Great First Interview Questions   107

• **XXVII** •

Don't Talk in an Interview   111

• **XXVIII** •

Handling Interviewer Concerns   115

• **XXIX** •

Show Something on Every Interview   120

CONTENTS

• **XXX** •

Ask to Do a Demonstration   123

• **XXXI** •

Don't Order Linguini with Marinara Sauce   128

• **XXXII** •

Look Like a Ballplayer   132

• **XXXIII** •

Make Them Feel Good   135

• **XXXIV** •

Flatter and Wow Them with
Your Interest   138

• **XXXV** •

How to Play Parlor Games   141

• **XXXVI** •

Always Ask for the Order   145

• **XXXVII** •

Always Send a Thank-you Note   150

CONTENTS

• **XXXVIII** •

Get Five Points Every Day   153

• **XXXIX** •

Keep a Daily Job-hunting To-do List   155

• **XL** •

The Job Seeker's Workday   158

• **XLI** •

Never Panic   160

• **XLII** •

Don't Ask for Directions   163

• **XLIII** •

"I" Is a Bad Word   166

• **XLIV** •

"Wind Me Up at Harvard!"   168

DON'T SEND A

RESUME

INTRODUCTION

You are reading this book because you now are looking for a job or are about to look for a job. You are just starting your search or have been in the job market for some time. You probably have anxiety; that's OK. You probably own or have read other books on getting a job, and that's OK. Some of those books are helpful and important. But this book is different. This book is about marketing and selling—the marketing and selling of yourself. Marketing and selling are business disciplines that many people haven't learned. These people may be students, manufacturing experts, accountants, lawyers, research scientists, human resource professionals, meeting planners, moms reentering the workforce, retired military personnel looking for a second career, fired CEOs, and even sales and marketing types.

Countless good people who are looking for a job—people who could make a positive contribution to any number of companies—are rejected daily by countless organizations. Why? One reason is that they look for a job the old-fashioned way. They rely on resumes and networking to land a job. They follow the "same old, same old" job-getting formula.

With some variation, the old formula is: Read books on how to get a job and how to write a resume and how to network, or get with an employment agency or outplacement firm. Then write a brilliant resume, write a compelling cover letter, print everything on exquisite stationery, mail resume and cover letter to the human resource departments of the Fortune 1000 (or some other list), take "how to interview" training, clear the calendar for the interviews. Finally, go to the mailbox, and from those companies that bothered to respond, read rejection form letters.

Microsoft doesn't sell software by sending a flyer

to ten million people and having employees call old contacts. Budweiser doesn't sell beer that way, and Procter & Gamble doesn't sell soap that way. Instead, the great marketing companies invest in innovation, create differentiated products, tailor the products to fill specific customer needs, and package and promote the products with clarity.

Every day, hirers in organizations—your customers, the buyers of *you*—see the same phrases in resume after resume. Every day, people on the network get replicated letters, ghostwritten by outplacement firms, from job seekers they don't know. Every day, potential hirers or influencers get resumes with cover letters that misspell their names. Every day, active hirers, or people with current hiring needs, get resumes and cover letters that contain nothing that is red-hot relevant to them. And every day, someone who is generous enough to meet a job seeker will hear that job seeker start the interview: "So what does your company do?"

Do the skills-listing and self-analysis exercises in

the other job-getting books. Understand your inner self, your drives, and your good and bad karma. Write down all your pros and cons.

Then do what's in this book and you will land your dream job, the one most suited to you. This book may not cut the time of your job search, but it will definitely reduce time wasted.

I

Don't Send
a Resume

A resume with a "for everyman" cover letter is
junk mail. A resume without a cover letter is
used to line the bottom of the birdcage. Most direct
mail hits the trash barrel between the mailbox and
the house. All unexpected and standard resumes go
from the IN box to the trash box. Some may generate a rejection form letter; most get ignored; 99.2
percent get tossed.

When a salesperson calls on a customer without
an appointment it is a cold call. Cold calls have a low
success rate. The customer may have absolutely no

need for the product, may not even be in the office. Telemarketers who call at dinnertime have a low success rate. The customer may be too busy to talk, may have absolutely no need for the product, or may not be home. Resumes that arrive without invitation have a low success rate. The person who receives the resume may have no need for an additional employee, may not even be the hiring person.

You are the product, and your resume is your sales literature. Super salespeople never send literature before meeting with a prospective customer. They know that sales literature sent prior to a needs analysis is odds-on to be irrelevant, off target, and unread. Super salespeople send literature after the first interview or bring it with them on follow-up calls. If the literature is not completely customized to the customer's needs, the salesperson highlights those product benefits most meaningful to the customer. Super salespeople create interest in their product and use sales literature to reaffirm and to leave a footprint, a product remembrance.

You must heed the example of the super salesperson. Your resume has much more validity and Velcro if the customer reads it after talking to you, hearing about you, or meeting you. This is particularly true if your resume is written for the hirer after you have interviewed the hirer. Your resume will validate your ability to deliver what the customer—the hirer—needs.

Turn junk mail into money mail. Don't send a resume without proper setup. If possible deliver your resume in person. Present your resume. Follow up with your resume.

II

Why Resumes Don't Sell

A young executive was interviewing with the company president. The president remarked, "Your resume is quite impressive." Disarmingly, the young executive answered, "It ought to be, I wrote it."

A funny response, maybe. A cocky response, probably. A candid response that deals directly with an underlying problem with resumes, definitely. No one writes a resume that states: "Weak manager. Afraid to make decisions. Afraid to change. Can't get along with people. Canned in last five jobs." Even though that might be closer to the truth for some managers, people write just the opposite. The resume is always biased to favor the candidate, and everyone knows it. Consequently, because it is inherently imbalanced no matter how skillfully crafted, the resume itself is a barrier that hirer and candidate must overcome.

Hirers expect resumes to represent one side of the candidate. Hirers expect embellishments in resumes. Hirers so expect an incomplete portrait that the resume is used only as a starting point in the interviewing and hiring process.

All resumes look alike. Regardless of the resume style—experience resume, chronological resume, functional resume—they all ultimately look the same. Selling yourself depends on getting noticed, standing apart, being different from everybody else. If at the outset you are represented *only* by your resume and your resume looks like everybody else's resume, then you look like everybody else.

The resume—any resume, all resumes—always acquires a personality of its own, which is often different from that of the person it glorifies. Resume-writing rules, resume structure, and the resume development process work together to produce, in effect, a new shadow persona. The modest take credit. The spare are verbose. The humble become egocentric. The literate use arcane jargon. The confident get cautious. The creative get common.

Resumes are too often an exercise in self-validation. This is particularly true for the seasoned manager—someone who has spent most of his or her career in one place—who now is uncomfortably in search of a new job. These resumes resonate with associated accomplishments, nearly a mirror for every success of the former organization for which the candidate worked. After reading such a resume, one wonders why the person needs to seek a new job.

Many resumes are too long. This is a plague on college campuses. Prospective faculty candidates (for hire or promotion) submit eight-page resumes (which they pedantically call curricula vitae) listing every paper they ever wrote, but only two sentences on teaching.

Your resume has two purposes: 1) to be intriguing enough to get you an interview; and 2) to reaffirm in a tailored way, after your interview, how hiring you solves the hirer's problem.

During your potential employer's workday, your resume competes with memos, reports, to-do lists, luncheon meetings, other resumes. Take a lesson from the gunfighter. His resume fit on his business card, yet it worked: "Paladin. Have gun. Will travel."

· III ·

The Job-getting Blueprint

- Target an organization.
- Research the organization.
- Write an impact letter to get an interview.
- Treat the interview as a sales call.
- Precall plan the interview.
- Dollarize your potential value to the organization.
- Bring something helpful to the company to the interview.
- Conduct a needs analysis during the interview.

- Write an individual resume for each target organization.
- Use the resume as interview follow-up sales literature.
- Send a thank-you note to each interviewer within one day of the interview.
- Precall plan each and every subsequent interview.

• IV •

Skip the Personnel Department

*T*he good people in the personnel or human resources department are not the buyers—the ultimate hirers. Unless you are seeking a job in the personnel department, these people are not making the hiring decision. The hirers are the managers in marketing, manufacturing, information technology, sales, and finance. The job seeker will be hired or rejected by the people for whom and with whom he or she would work. The actual hirers are your customers—the people to whom you must sell yourself.

The personnel department is a screen, a gate-keeper. Part of their job is to keep unwanted, un-expected, unrequested resumes from cluttering managers' desks. Unless the personnel people are alerted to a specific hiring need, they do not care-fully review and study resumes and job applications looking for the next superstar. In fact, the personnel department views most nonspecific resumes and job applications as time wasters.

Even when the people in human resources are looking for a certain type of potential employee, their selection process starts with rejection. Particu-larly when a job opportunity is advertised, person-nel people often face stacks of resumes to review. Their goal is to dramatically reduce the stack. They scan resumes looking for reasons to reject candi-dates. Resumes are tossed because of a candidate's school, affiliations, geographical location, or job his-tory. Resumes are rejected because the reviewer is weary or thinks he has already found the perfect candidate, or because he misreads the write-up.

People in human resources, especially early in

the hiring process, hire by the book. The book is the written job description. Good candidates are routinely rejected because their background doesn't seem to precisely mirror the job description. The human resources department wrote the job description, or participated in the writing, so anything in the resume that is even slightly off the job description is cause for rejection. The actual hirers are more flexible, meaning that they commonly hire "talent" and refit the job to match the talent.

Starting your selling approach at the personnel department means you don't know who your customer really is. It means you don't know why the company should hire you. It means you don't know who in the company will benefit from hiring you. Consequently, your cover letter will be general, and your resume will be non-tailored. You are then dependent on one person in personnel to properly interpret your resume, translate your resume into relevant value to the company, and then voluntarily send your resume to the head of information systems with a note saying, "Hire this digital video expert immediately." That doesn't happen.

The human resources department is important. They are expert interviewers. They give and interpret tests. They handle all post-hire administration. Their opinions are valuable and considered. But, almost always, the hiring decision is made elsewhere.

Start selling yourself to that person who will recognize and need the value you will bring to the organization. Start with the CEO or the head of manufacturing or the vice-president of sales. If the job opportunity is advertised and the hiring company is named and the job looks right for you, use the advertisement as a lead. Study the company. Do your homework. Send the proper hiring person an impact letter, and get an interview.

The personnel department is much more helpful to you *after* you've been hired.

• V •

The Job Seeker's Marketing Mix

Getting a job consists of marketing and selling yourself to a company. This is the same thing as a company's marketing and selling its products to its customers. The techniques used to market a product are collectively called the "marketing mix." The marketing mix is the marketer's toolbox. Marketers use some or all of the tools in varying ways and in differing proportions. How marketers use the marketing mix is a function of selling goals, skills, targeting of customers' needs, budgets, competition. The marketing mix includes advertising, publicity, packaging, pricing, market research, direct mail, and numerous other disciplines.

You must consider all possible pieces of the marketing mix in marketing yourself. Your marketing plan for yourself will be a recipe of the ingredients in the marketing mix.

Your Marketing Mix

ADVERTISING When someone who knows you, or knows of you, recommends you to a potential employer, that is word-of-mouth advertising. Ask influential people you know to spread the word.

DATABASE MARKETING Build your people file with letters, press and magazine clippings of interest, e-mails, and phone calls—and use it.

DIRECT MARKETING Sending a letter to a hiring person in a target company with a message tailored to the company is effective direct mail.

LEAD GENERATION Identifying a hiring company, getting an introduction, or getting a referral are sales leads. Networking, want ads, and industry publications are good sources.

MARKET RESEARCH Use the Internet, the library, publications, the street, and the phone to learn all you can about the target company, its industry, and its people.

MEDIA PLAN Use the Internet to contact companies and respond to companies. Put up a personalized web site.

PRICING The marketplace usually sets the price—the compensation for your job—but showing your economic value and dollarizing your impact is crucial to the hiring person.

PUBLICITY Write articles, contact organizers for associations, and give speeches on what you know.

Put writers, reporters, editors in your database. Let them know you are available for a quote.

SEGMENTATION The world of organizations can be segmented by geography, industry, size, customers, culture, age, whether they are private or public, profit or not-for-profit, and countless variations. Your forty-mile radius is the first step (see Draw a Forty-mile Circle, Chapter IX).

SELLING You are selling yourself. There are books on selling. Read them.

TRADESHOWS Job fairs are trade shows for hiring employers. Industry trade shows are where companies selling to common customers present themselves. Visit your target companies at trade shows.

· VI ·

The Job Seeker's Glossary

Getting a job consists of marketing, selling, and promotion—of yourself. You have to understand the jargon of job seeking and translate that jargon into meaningful marketing clues. Don't let the commonly used language lull you into a by-the-book job-seeking approach. For example, all the experts extoll the virtues of the perfect resume, yet people who do the hiring by instinct and experience know that resumes are not perfect. Resumes are simply sales literature for the job seeker. The interviewer is the buyer, and you are the salesperson. The job interview is a sales call on that customer. That sales call is precious, and must be meticulously pre-planned and practiced.

THE JARGON	WHAT THE JARGON MEANS
Candidate	Product the company is buying
Compensation	Price they want to pay for the product
Cover letter	Direct mail advertising
Hiring company	Bill Smith and Anne Jones (Companies don't hire; people do.)
Interviewer	Your customer
Job	Solution to a company problem
Job description	A starting point to determine what the company needs
Job expectation	Cash return on compensation, on the investment in candidate
Job interview	Sales call
Job seeker	Salesperson (selling yourself)
Personality tests	"Do you fit?" tests

Don't Send a Resume

Resume	Sales literature
Stress interview	Parlor games
Want ad	Clues about company

• VII •

You Are a
Box of Cereal

You are a stamping press, a gearbox, a software package, a centrifuge, or an electric motor. You are a box of corn flakes competing with every other cereal to catch the eye of the customer, to get plucked off the shelf, to get purchased.

You are a product.

When companies hire, they make an investment. Hiring someone—paying compensation—is no different from buying a lathe, a copy machine, or a forklift. Hiring someone is precisely like buying any productivity-improving product. Just as the hiring company wants its investment in a new retail store design to increase sales, so too it wants its investment in people to increase sales. Just as the hiring company expects its investment in new CAD/CAM software to reduce production costs, it wants its investment in new people to eliminate scrap and waste.

You are a product and the employer is the customer, the buyer. You are a product the customer will buy if the customer feels good about you, and if you solve a problem. As with a box of cereal, the customer will feel good about you if he or she likes your packaging. And your packaging, because you are you, is how you look, listen, learn, laugh. The customer will feel good about you if you fit the organization's culture, if you have "chemistry," and if you ask thoughtful questions. The customer will feel good about you if you are genuine, if you have done your homework, and if you are enthusiastic about betting some of your life on the hiring company. More importantly, however, the customer—the hiring organization—will only hire you if they think you can solve their problem, if you fill their need. You are a product the customer will buy if you are affordable, and if in solving his problem the customer will earn more from your work than the amount of money you will be paid for that work.

You are not a robot, but you will be purchased as if you were a robotic assembly machine.

VIII

Always Dollarize Yourself

Dollarizing is calculating, in dollars and cents, what you are worth to your customer, the hiring organization. If you can increase sales by $600,000, you are worth some of the profit on the $600,000. If you can reduce scrap and waste by $95,000, you are worth some of the $95,000. If you can reduce bank loan interest by 0.5 percent, you are worth some of that interest savings. The more dollarized value the hiring company sees in you, the higher the probability you will be hired.

Jobs exist to create value. The purpose of a job is

to directly or indirectly get and keep customers. This is true for profit and nonprofit organizations. Value is created by increasing revenues, reducing costs, and innovating new products and services. If the job does not create value it will ultimately disappear. If the cost for the job exceeds the economic value the job creates, the job will either be eliminated or replaced with a less expensive alternative. If the job is known to create value but the person in the job is inadequate, then—of the job and the person—only the job will survive. The cost of a job includes recruitment, compensation, benefits, training, office space, tools, samples, mistakes, and supervision. You must create more value than your cost.

Most organizations have a sense of what a job costs; that means they generally know what they have to pay and understand the actual costs—which include benefits, training, and such—are considerably higher than the base compensation. Some organizations have a general idea of the economic value they expect from their investment in the job, but are never sure they will get that return. Consequently, the hiring people are always trying to evaluate each job candidate's potential to create value. To help the hiring people choose you, you must dollarize yourself. You must quantify for the organization the economic value you can potentially deliver.

Because the purpose of every job is to create value, you must, in pre-interview homework, determine how the job in question creates value for your target organization. For example, a salesperson creates value by generating sales revenue. A purchasing agent creates value by acquiring quality components at true net lower costs. A construction project manager creates value by ensuring that the building is finished on time, avoiding cost overruns. A maintenance person creates value by keeping the machinery running, eliminating costly downtime. The hotel housekeeper creates value by making the hotel room so comfortable that the customer returns. In these examples, the sales candidate's value is some function of the $2,000,000 in revenues she claims she will deliver. The prospective purchasing agent will show how he can save the company $1,000,000 by buying gaskets that reduce warranty claims. The project manager will demonstrate to his future employer that his computer-based scheduling skills will save $5,000,000 in possible penalties. The maintenance person will show that every hour of downtime avoided is worth $87,000 to the hiring company. And the hotel housekeeper will show that superbly cleaned hotel rooms create a loyal customer who will return three more nights at $150 a night.

Every job can be dollarized. Every job has value. You must carefully consider how the job you want creates value. In your interviews ask questions and answer questions in such a way that your dollarized value becomes evident.

To illustrate . . .

CANDIDATE FOR CHIEF TECHNOLOGY OFFICER: What financial problems are your present systems causing you?

INTERVIEWER: It appears that we have problems with on-time deliveries and ensuring adequate inventories.

CANDIDATE: How much customer dissatisfaction and lost sales is the lack of proper inventory costing you?

INTERVIEWER: We're not sure, but it is significant.

CANDIDATE: Would it be reasonable to assume that properly designed and managed systems could save the company several million dollars over the next twenty-four months?

INTERVIEWER: Yes.

CANDIDATE: Based on experience, an initiative to tie your systems together will eliminate the problem and recapture five million dollars in lost sales. I can make this happen for you. Would you like to give it a try?

The CTO candidate dollarized his value, and asked for the order. You must do the same.

IX

Draw a Forty-mile Circle

*L*ike all marketing efforts getting a job requires proactive, hard work. It is not enough to answer want ads and blanket the world with resumes. Operating under the correct assumption that good companies are always looking for impact players, you must take control of your destiny and seek out and find one good company. The company may or may not be in the market for you. The company may not know it needs you. The company won't even know who you are. That matters not a wit. If you can improve a company's top line or improve its economics in any way, you will be in demand.

If you know a company for whom you would like to work, target them first. If you do not know any target companies, pick one or two or three cities or towns where you would like to live. Then get out a map, and with the desired town as a centerpoint, use a compass and draw a circle with a forty- or fifty-mile radius. This is the area where you will begin your job search.

Next, go to the library or use the Internet, and begin researching the reference books that detail the businesses in your search area. Good reference materials include the various Dun and Bradstreet listings, the *Standard Directory of International Advertisers and Advertising Agencies: The International Red Book*, and the state-published directories of companies. Unless you have a burning desire to work in one industry, be totally indiscriminant as to potential companies. Don't negatively prejudge a company or industry, assuming, for example, that the products are too technical or that the company sounds boring or that it is too big or too small. Every company has appeal to someone. Obviously, you can eliminate any companies that are in an industry that is distasteful to you, or that sell products that you find personally offensive. Identify five or six companies which, for any reason, appeal to you in some way.

These companies are where you must focus your efforts. Learn all you can about these companies. Read all their sales literature and annual reports, if available. Visit their web site. Buy their product(s) if possible. Talk to retailers, distributors, and customers. Research your target company's competitors. See what's been published about your company, its industry, its competitors. Then, based on what you have learned, write an impact letter to the CEO of the company outlining five or six ways the company could be improved. A good letter will get you an interview.

If the first forty-mile circle is a bust, draw another one in a different place. There are lots of companies out there that will hire you when they learn how you can improve their top or bottom line.

· X ·

How to Research a Target Company

Y ou have identified a company for which you want to work. Your first objective is to get an interview—a sales call—with the highest-level decision maker in the company. To get that interview you must demonstrate how you can benefit the company. To determine how you can benefit the company requires diligent and resourceful homework and research. Do your homework as if you were the CEO of the company and were thinking, "How can I improve this company? How can I grow sales, increase profits, cut costs, speed up innovation?" With these guiding thoughts, the goal of your research of the company is to discover ideas, suggestions, observations that could lead to economic improvement.

Whether your expertise is in manufacturing, sales, accounting, research and development (R&D), or anything at all, conduct your research as if you were in charge of that function; and also answer the question, "How can I improve the production process, in order to shorten deliveries, improve product quality, reduce scrap?" Or, "How can I improve marketing, finance, human resources?" and so on.

There are numerous sources of information about nearly every company. Information is in the library, in stores, in retired employees, in databases, on the Internet. You want to learn all you can about the company, its people, its products, its markets, its competition, and its future.

If you follow the research routes (outlined here) you will learn more about the company than is known by most of the company's employees. No other candidate competing for the same job will do this research.

1. Call the company and request sales literature, annual reports, technical information, product brochures, price lists. You may have to say you are a potential customer, a possible investor, or a consultant doing research for a client interested in buying product. These are all possibly true statements.

2. If the product is available at retail, visit the stores. Buy the product if affordable, use the product. Talk to store personnel. Get the names of the salespeople who sell to the stores. Get the store's opinion on the company, ideas for new products, what competitors are doing.

3. If the product is sold through a distribution system, visit a local distributor. Ask about the quality of the product, the skill and training of the sales force, new market opportunities, technical support.

4. If the product is sold directly to customers, call some. Ask the customers' opinions on delivery, reputation, innovation, sales force, warranty issues.

5. Call the company's 800 number. Analyze the experience.

6. Call the company's advertising agency and talk to the account executive responsible for the client. Ask where you can see or hear the advertising. Find out at what trade shows the company exhibits.

7. There are magazines for nearly every industry. Call the magazines and get articles on the company. Whether or not your target company is a member of a trade association, there are often such associations that can provide good information.

8. Talk to salespeople and employees of the company and of its competitors. Talk to ex-employees of the company and competitors.

9. Get the competitors' literature.

10. Call suppliers to the company and to the industry. If the company makes chewing gum, talk to people who sell flavors. If the company makes the entire product in-house, talk to people who supply services such as printing or sales automation.

11. Lexis-Nexis is a good Internet search engine to use when your target company's name has appeared in print.

When doing your research, constantly ask about problems, changes in the marketplace, areas to improve, trends that affect the company, new product ideas.

You now are prepared to write a compelling impact letter to the company's CEO. Develop an effective show piece for your interviews. Craft thoughtful needs-analysis questions for your interviews. Then hit the road running when you are hired.

· XI ·

Look Where They Ain't

When the fabled bank robber Willie Sutton (1901–1980) was asked why he robbed banks, his street-savvy answer was, "That's where the money is." When Hall-of-Fame baseball player Wee Willie Keeler (1872–1923) was asked to explain his batting prowess, he philosophized, "Keep a clear eye and hit 'em where they ain't." To paraphrase the wisdom of the Willies: When you are looking for a job, look where they ain't. Look for a job where no other job seeker looks. That's where the money is. Here are seven unorthodox places to look for a job:

1. Venture capitalists, leverage buyout firms, and equity investor firms

These companies make financial investments in companies, hoping to sell the companies later for great profit. The people who work in these firms are financial experts. They are not operating managers. They usually know very little about manufacturing, marketing, or distribution. They do have a good eye for management, and are skilled people pickers. They are always on the lookout for seasoned managers, particularly for any of their portfolio companies in trouble. Some of these companies will put a proven executive on their payroll until a situation arises where the executive can move into an operating role.

2. Small companies

Small companies (revenues less than $25,000,000) are often better places to work than large companies. People who have worked in big companies or who have strong educational backgrounds commonly overlook the world of small business. Small-company personnel are closer to customers and therefore better value the efforts that get and keep customers than do large companies. Small companies generally offer more job security, because hiring is done less frequently, with great care, and with an important need to fill. Small companies are competitive in compensation, up to a $175,000 to $200,000 ceiling. And if you are good enough to move a large company an inch, then you can move a small company a mile—for which the rewards are fair.

3. Go East Young Woman!

China is the world's next economic superpower. The opportunities for workers and managers grow greater by the day. Good US companies, good Chinese companies, and good foreign companies are looking for people willing to invest in a China-based career, willing to learn Mandarin, and who see the planet as their marketplace.

4. *¡Aprende un poco de español!*

Cuba will become open to US businesses. Either Castro will relinquish power or Congress will repeal US sanctions, or both. Any new Cuban leader will understand the futility of Castro economics, and will move to a rapprochement with the United States. Cuba is becoming a more vibrant marketplace, full of current and future opportunities in tourism, banking, hotels, casinos, crops, ranching, restaurants, and sports. Foreign investment is moving into Cuba. Even the dimmest of US politicians now afraid of losing Cuba to communism will understand we can't lose Cuba to foreign capitalism. If you would like to live in the Caribbean, swim along the greatest beaches in the world, participate in the rebirth of a "cool" country, then Cuba should be on your list. Consider resort developers, international bankers—even McDonald's. They all will be in Cuba. Study *Español*!

5. Trust and estate bankers and lawyers

A trust is a legal entity formed to look after and protect economic assets. Sometimes the economic asset is a family-owned business. The business can be in a trust for various reasons, but it still needs managers. Large banks with trust departments regularly have such businesses in their portfolio. Bankers in trust departments and lawyers who specialize in trusts and estates can be a good source of leads to companies needing better management.

6. Commercial loan officers

Commercial loan officers are bankers who make loans to companies. If those companies get in trouble the loans are at risk. Commercial lenders don't want their loans in default, and they look to management to steer the company properly. Consequently, commercial bankers can be an excellent source of leads to companies needing better management.

7. Bankruptcy trustees and lawyers

Certain of the bankruptcy laws are in place to protect failing companies, to give companies an opportunity to revive and eventually pay their creditors. Companies that have a chance to emerge from bankruptcy are stronger economically than they were previously. And almost always, the old management is gone. Bankruptcy trustees (judges) and lawyers who specialize in bankruptcy can be an excellent source of leads for companies needing new management.

Looking for a new job where no one else is looking increases your odds for success.

Write an
Impact Letter

*T*here is always a job in a good organization for an impact player. An impact player is someone who can quickly improve the economics of a company. An impact player is someone who can bring in customers, energize the sales force, restructure an under-performing department, speed up the innovation process, solve the late shipment problem, or physically move the manufacturing facility to a lower cost area. An impact player also is someone who will do the necessary but noxious tasks no one else wants to do. An impact player is someone who will get

their hands dirty, pick up a shovel and start shovel-
ing, open the store early and close late, deliver product on their way home, deal tirelessly with irate
customers, and make a service call on Christmas
Eve. Good executives in good companies want to
hire impact players. To get the attention of the CEO
in your target company, write him or her a letter
that demonstrates your ability to impact the company.

Research the company exhaustively, constantly
looking for areas where your skills and experience
might be of benefit to them. While reading the company's literature; trying the products; talking to customers, competitors, and suppliers you will discover
good business opportunities or challenges, or both.
Dollarize the value of those business opportunities.
To dollarize is to calculate the dollar value to the
company of the business opportunities you have dis-
covered. Write a one-page letter to the CEO of the
company or the highest-ranking relevant hiring
executive. Pinpoint four or five opportunities for

the company where your expertise and ideas will be useful. If the letter is carefully written, and your proposed opportunities are reasonably feasible, you will, in most cases, at least get an interview. If, for whatever reason, the company can't hire you, the person you interviewed may have other good contacts. If you don't get hired full-time, you might be offered a consulting assignment to work on one of the opportunities you described in your impact letter. A consulting assignment is a great way for you and the company to evaluate each other. Doing well may lead to a full-time position.

It is far better to do the hard work of producing five impact letters that get great results than to send out five hundred resumes that generate five hundred rejections. A good impact letter demonstrates your potential to make an impact.

Impact Letter: Example #1
Written by a person with manufacturing skills to the CEO.

Dear Mr. Day:

You have a great company and I have spent some time studying it. Based on my research, which includes observing your products in use by your customers, there are four things that would have a positive economic impact on your business.

1. Customers complain that Product A occasionally loses hydraulic fluid, creating one hour of costly downtime while being repaired. The problem can be solved with a redesigned lip seal. I know how to get that done.

2. Based on a description of your factory floor layout, there would be considerable savings to you if you adapt the Toyota motor car's one-piece flow production method to your manufacturing process.

3. Such a process will also result in reduced factory floor space usage, and less inventory of vendor parts.

4. Customers say your lead time on shipments is now sixteen weeks. There are a number of ways to reduce that lead time.

If I don't hear from you, I will follow up to discuss how to make these ideas a reality.

Manufacturingly Yours,
Baldwin A. Ward

P.S. One customer suggested a product improvement that might be a good new product. It is a neat idea.

Impact Letter: Example #2

A letter from a sales candidate to the Vice-President of Sales.

Dear Mr. Baker:

You have a great company and I have spent some time studying it. Based on my research, which includes observing your products in use by your customers, there are four things that would have a positive economic impact on your business.

1. I visited twenty of your customer stores. Product A was available in fourteen stores.

The other six stores are good target accounts as they move considerable volume. With persistence I can get your product on their shelves.

2. In addition, only two stores were using your display materials, and they were getting good results. We could take the experience of those two stores and educate every customer to the sales-generating potential of proper display.

3. One customer said she would be willing to stock all of your sku's but she can't find anyone to show her how to merchandise the line. Her concern might represent an opportunity for a national planogram promotion.

4. Your competitor is test marketing a new product in Boston. I have some verbatims from the retailers and a few of their customers as to how the new product is doing. We could discuss some ideas on what you might do in response.

If I don't hear from you, I will follow up to propose how to make these ideas a reality.

Sellingly Yours,
Ewell C. Rezultz

P.S. There is a new channel of distribution available to you. This channel could add 5 percent volume to your top line.

• XIII •

Write
Boomerang Letters

*T*he Australian bushman hunts with the boomerang. The job seeker also hunts with the boomerang—in letter form. The boomerang letter is used to answer "positions available" and want ads. The boomerang letter flies the want ad words—the copy—back to the writer of the ad. This is a compelling sales technique.

Companies that advertise job openings put a lot of thought into the ad copy. The ads try to attract the right kind of person and screen out the wrong. The ads must compete with the ads of other companies. It is not unusual for a want ad to be a product of several authors or contributors. These ads are important. They cost money to run in the media. They cost money to create (there are advertising agencies that specialize solely in writing these kinds of ads). The hiring company must not only invest money to write and run these ads, they also invest themselves into the ads. The ads are surrogates for company recruiters, hirers, and spokespeople. The ad copy is sometimes an accurate reflection of the company's culture. Sometimes they overhype and oversell the job and the company; but almost always there is some pride of authorship and a hopeful satisfaction in the effectiveness of the wording. Flatter the person who wrote the ad with your response letter. Echo the author's words and intent. Your letter should be a mirror of the ad. The ad writer's words should return to her like a boomerang. When she reads your letter she will see some of herself. She will think, "This person seems to fit the description. This person gets it." Your on-target response will validate the ad copy, giving the copywriter a positive return on her emotional investment in creating the ad.

When you get the interview, your job will be to prove to the company that they will also get a financial return on their investment in hiring you. Boomerang letters are like the boomerang—sophisticated simplicity.

Ad for Property Manager: Example #1

Regional Real Estate Investment Company seeks property manager with five years of experience. Responsible for overall management and leasing of a 25-property portfolio. Properties include industrial, office, and multifamily housing. Experience in various properties desirable. Development oversight and acquisition due diligence a plus. Excellent written and verbal communication skills required. Proven background in financial analysis a must. Please send resume to Bill Farley, Vice-President of Operations.

Corresponding Boomerang Letter to Bill Farley,
Vice-President of Operations.

Dear Mr. Farley:

As a seasoned real estate property manager, my typical workday starts with an inspection of rubbish removal at our industrial locations, moves to maintenance issues at our office buildings, and concludes with a review of past-due rents at our multifamily houses. At least once a month, as part of our continuing property acquisition, I provide the financial analysis piece of the due diligence. Membership on the development oversight and leasing committee for a number of properties in our portfolio is a transferable experience.

If you are looking for a manager who can wear many hard hats and keep the buildings profitable, we should talk. If I don't hear from you first, at 940-678-1234, you will receive a follow-up call.

Sincerely yours,
Lisa Land

P.S. Relocation, relocation, relocation is not a problem for me.

Ad for Marketing Services Coordinator: Example #2

ABC Printing Corp. is seeking an experienced, career-minded individual to become a key player on its marketing team. The successful candidate will possess strong skills in math, organization, and communication, both verbal and written. Must be computer literate. Experience in the printing industry is a definite plus. Ability to interact with customers, outside sales, and factory people at all levels in a high-powered environment is key. Strong interpersonal skills are essential. Position is heavily focused in customer service. Please send resume and salary history to Harry Viens, Director of Customer Service.

Corresponding Boomerang Letter to Harry Viens, Director of Customer Service

Dear Mr. Viens:

If you are looking for a marketing services coordinator who is willing to work hard, is a team player, and who will flourish in a high-powered, high-energy company, please consider me for that position. Customer service is one of the most important functions in a company. Ensuring good customer service means having the ability to communicate with customers, and to coordinate the efforts of outside salespeople and printing-plant personnel to deliver what the customer wants.

You can quickly evaluate my computer and verbal skills in an interview. You may reach me at 297-399-1101, or I will call to follow up.

Printingly yours,
Byers R. Phirst

P.S. My career has been, and will be, in a marketing company that understands customer focus.

• XIV •
Send a
Resu-letter

There are occasions in the job-seeking process when you should send a "resu-letter." For example, a help-wanted ad may ask applicants to send a resume and salary history. Send a resu-letter. A recruiter or another intermediary may have set up a job interview for you that requires some pre-info. Send a resu-letter.

A resu-letter is a proxy for your formal, structured resume. A resu-letter is a readable, humanized summary of those highlights in your background that are relevant to the customer, the hirer. A resu-letter enables you to present your experience in a non-resume format. You can mix biographical and chronological information in a way not seen in standard resume styles.

Your resu-letter should demonstrate some understanding of the target company. Your resu-letter should, like the boomerang letter, reflect some of the hiring company's want-ad copy. A resu-letter has more credibility then a resume because it is not a resume. Whereas the reader knows a resume might exaggerate one's accomplishments, the resu-letter gets a more forgiving read. In this job-getting process, the resu-letter is often followed by your resume. In effect, the resu-letter tees up your resume, and the two documents reinforce each other, strengthening your case.

If nothing else, your resu-letter will stand out as different amongst the pile of standard resumes. This will give you an edge.

A Sample Resu-letter:

A letter from a candidate for Research and Development manager to the company president.

Dear Ms. La Plant:

In response to your request for personal and business background, this letter summarizes relevant experience. Presently, I am responsible for a team of six scientists working to uncover more commercial applications for our core technologies. The position includes goal setting, brainstorming, work supervision, motivation, hiring, training, and firing. This job represents my fourth promotion in nine years. The cost center budget is $1.6 million.

Prior to joining ABS Corp. I received a Ph.D. in biochemistry from Georgia Tech. My undergraduate degree (BS, Chemistry) and my MS in Industrial Management were both completed at Lehigh University in Pennsylvania. Professional memberships include the Association of Chemical Engineers and the American Management Association.

Colleagues and annual reviews would probably

characterize my management style as outcome focused and open-minded. In an interview you will be able to augment this work snapshot in as much detail as you would like. Thank you.

Researchingly yours,

George Patent

P.S. My group has developed twenty-two concepts with a sales value of $6,600,000. We can discuss this as well.

• XV •

Be a Fish out of Water

This story is advertising industry lore. It is said that one of the giants of advertising got his first job working in the mailroom of a Madison Avenue agency. He was a creative fellow and wanted desperately to become at least a copywriter. He applied internally—through the personnel department—for a job in the creative department. But this ad agency was flooded with resumes from the best and the brightest; why even consider a kid from the mailroom? And the agency didn't. Time after time, the mailroom boy's traditional, by-the-book, according-to-policy, follow-the-rules, do-it-the-company-way application was rejected, barely considered.

He knew a challenge facing the art directors and copywriters was how to make their ads stand out, get noticed amongst all the ads and commercials competing for the fickle buyer's attention. He knew that getting favorable buyer attention was what clients paid his agency to do, and ad success led to the agency's financial success. The kid from the mail-room reasoned he had the same problem as did the creative people: how to design an ad for his product (i.e., himself) so different, so unexpected, that it would grab attention despite that pile of competing ads, the other resumes. What would it take, he schemed and noodled, to get the heads of the agency to notice his flair, and to give him a chance to write ads that would keep clients and get new clients?

He had access to everyone's office—he delivered the mail. The mail boy targeted his customer, the creative director of the advertising agency. The mail boy learned that the creative director appreciated surprise, breakthrough thinking, and getting products noticed. One morning, at the top of his mail pile, the creative director of the advertising agency found a package of something wrapped in newspaper. The creative director unwrapped the newspaper to find a big fish, fully five pounds from head to tail. Spread on his fine desk, giving him an unflinching fish eye, lay a bass or snapper or snook. The page that held the fish, a bit wrinkled and scaly, was a newspaper from his agency. Enclosed was a note: "I'm like a fish out of water down here in the mailroom. I can make ads that get noticed. Why don't you give me a try?" Signed, The Mailroom Boy.

Audacious? Perhaps. Funny? A bit. Clever? For sure. Risky? What's to lose? Attention getting? Aren't most fish stories?

The mailroom boy became a storied ad man, ultimately founding a highly successful agency that bore his name.

In a good company there is always a job for a moneymaker, a revenue producer, a customer getter. Don't tell them, show them. And you need not be a Pisces to get noticed.

· XVI ·

Don't Play
Resume Roulette

*F*looding the marketplace with resumes is a low-risk, low-return gamble. The chances of finding a job are small, and the chance of finding the dream job that perfectly fits you depends on pure luck. A mass mailing of resumes is playing resume roulette.

No two companies are the same. Each company has its own culture, its own management structure, and its own brands. Each company has different hiring profiles and different job needs. Even companies in the same industry selling to the same customers are different. Competing companies employ different business strategies, different financial models, and different distribution approaches. Coca-Cola and Pepsi-Cola, for example, are polar opposites; each management team spends every minute trying, in fact, to create even greater differences and distinctions between the two companies. Because every hiring organization is different, and because every hiring individual is different, you can't sell your unique talents with a cookie-cutter approach. One size does not fit all. A common resume used for all companies is just that—common! To be noticed, you need a resume that connects with the reader. To connect with a resume reader your resume must address the hiring needs, wants, and concerns of that reader. Your resume must be written and customized to reflect the needs of each separate hiring organization.

In the selling of products there is an endless array of marketing strategies and approaches. One strategy is known as mass marketing. Mass marketing is typically used to sell a popular product such as detergent to a mass market of, say, homemakers. This is an efficient approach, as measured in the cost to reach each potential customer. It is not as effective as segmented marketing, where the seller sells one special formula of detergent to a nurse's uniform-cleaning customer and another detergent to customers who only use cold water. The most effective marketing, though at higher cost, is one-to-one marketing. This is when the seller customizes the product offering to meet the needs of a single buyer. This is how automobile makers will eventually sell you cars on the Internet. You pick the color, options, and style. The car companies will build the car you want and ship it where you want it. One-to-one is the marketing strategy you must use to get a job. You must craft your talent and experience and genius so that it fills the needs of your customer, the hiring organization. Your resume must be read as the perfect solution to that company's problem.

If the company's problem is lagging sales, demonstrate how you ring the cash register. If the problem is a lack of innovation, your resume will reference the science fair prizes you won in high school. If the company's problem is high costs, your resume will show how you reduce waste and improve productivity. A company having trouble delivering its products on time wants to know how your three summers' worth of experience selling hotdogs at Foxy Franks in Willimantic, Connecticut, where service and speed under pressure matter, can translate into efficiency. Don't write one resume and send it to five or fifty or five hundred companies. Rather, do your homework on five or fifty or five hundred companies and write five or fifty or five hundred unique resumes tailored to the needs of each individual company.

Fifty different companies, fifty different resumes.

• XVII •

Nontraditional Clues for Writing a Resume

Since everyone knows that the resume genre falls somewhere between fiction and nonfiction and is certainly an exercise in creative writing, here are some clues for a more distinctive resume (if you need one).

1. A company-tailored resume with an interviewer-tailored cover letter, used as a follow-up to an interview, is the most effective resume.

2. A resume tailored to a company is better than a general resume with a tailored cover letter.

3. In a tailored resume the bottom of your resume should be on top. The "personal" section in a typical resume is a way of humanizing and distinguishing yourself.

4. In a general resume the "personal" section is risky. Your white-water rapids hobby might be a recurring nightmare for the reader.

5. You can stretch your experience, you can creatively position your experience, you can imply great importance to your experience, but you cannot lie. If you worked as a summer intern stuffing and sending envelopes with questionnaires on the construction industry you can claim: "Responsibility for the implementation of a major market research program to identify new product and acquisition opportunities in the construction industry." You cannot say, "Project Research Manager for ABC advertising agency's study on the construction industry."

6. Eliminate all self-serving self-descriptions. It's embarrassing to read (and to write!) phrases

such as "passion for customer service," "strategic thinker with long-term vision," "proven leadership," "results-oriented," and "ability to rise to new challenges." Be different. Don't write this kind of cotton candy.

7. Instead use facts, incidents, and numbers to reveal your good qualities. Instead of saying, "consistently demonstrated superior leadership," write, "weapons officer on Navy submarine commanding a team of twelve sailors on four North Atlantic tracking missions." Or write, "Headed two-year task force to battle US government's FTC complaint against two corporate acquisitions. Won both cases."

8. Eliminate all organization- and industry-specific language. Replace with plain English. For example, instead of "Received key Wheely Bird Award," write, "Received outstanding manager award." Don't write, "Implemented an ROBMS system." Do write, "Implemented state-of-the-art budgeting and financial system."

9. Concentrate your resume on your last five to eight years. Position that experience to match the job needs of your targeted company. No one cares about your accomplishments of twenty years ago.

10. Drop the "affiliations" section of your resume. Affiliations and memberships can be controversial. An unintended and unwanted consequence of affiliation listings is that otherwise normal and worthy memberships can create negatives. Hirers may, for example, see negatives in Mensa (elitist), the Boy Scouts of America (discriminatory), Knights of Columbus (religious), Hartford Wanderers Rugby Football Club (ruffian).

11. Send a picture of yourself in action: making a presentation, receiving an award, loading a truck, selling a newspaper. The right picture for the right position may be all the resume you need.

A high-school senior was applying to St. Lawrence University in upstate New York.

She learned that St. Lawrence was proud of a famous alumnus, the movie actor Kirk Douglas. The story was that the dirt-poor Douglas arrived on campus in a pickup truck and was admitted. The high-school senior sent to the admissions office a photo of herself wearing a St. Lawrence sweatshirt and sitting in the back of a pickup. She was accepted.

No one else will send a photo.

12. Skip the "Summary." This section is always such puffery that no one buys any of it. They often read like this: "Unique executive; acknowledged as an expert; particularly adept at identifying opportunities; consistently successful; consistently accomplished the mission; consistent leadership; demonstrated track record; expertise in directing; achieved dramatic growth; and superior team building ability." What hirer reads such stuff, throws down the resume, shouts "alleluia," skips the interviews, and hires the person by e-mail? None.

{75}

13. The only acceptable "job objective" is to directly or indirectly help the company profitably get and keep customers. That objective is the only purpose of a job.

14. Do not use "I" in your resume. Write in the third person, not the first person (cover letters and resu-letters, although written in the first person, must minimize "I" and should use "you").

15. Your resume should clearly and persuasively answer the question, "Why should this organization hire me?"

16. Never write a resume that exceeds two pages in length. Resumes longer than two pages tell the hirer that you are overly impressed with yourself, that you can't prioritize, that you don't get to the point—and that on the job your memos or reports will be snore bait.

• XVIII •

No One Cares about Your Job Objective

Resume after resume starts as follows:

"Job objective: to capitalize on twenty years of operations management, strategic planning, and international sales by obtaining a senior executive position in a growing company."

"Job Objective: to secure a general management position in a growing, innovative company that will benefit from fifteen years of hands-on experience building businesses and structuring successful start-ups."

Employers don't care what you want: They only care about what they want.

Employers don't care about your job objective: They only care about their objective. If your so-called job objective is different from what the potential employer has in mind, why should he or she keep reading your resume? If, as in the examples above, your job objective is so general that it has no relevance, why should the hirer keep reading? The traditional "job objective" segment of a resume is just more camouflage to express how great you are. Most hirers are inured to the self-promotion in resumes and are looking for facts, relevant experience, and some kind of spark. The only correct "job objective" is that which expressly states what the customer, the employing organization wants. This personalized job objective will resonate. You find out what the customer wants through homework, research, and needs analysis. For example, you are applying for a job as a teacher in a town's elementary school system. You research the school, the town, and the board of education. You talk to some parents, attend a PTO meeting, read the last few years of the local paper. You determine that your target customer, the school superintendent, is concerned that the kids are not getting a good foundation in math. Instead of using the traditional resume job objective approach, you write an impact letter to the superintendent.

Dear Mrs. Dawson-Brown:

If you are interested in motivating your K–6 students to love numbers and do well in arithmetic, then I am your "math magician." With my assortment of original classroom games, puzzlers, and team competitions, your kids will look forward to math class more than lunch and recess. Here is your winning equation: Add me to your team and subtract math malaise.

Mathematically Yours,
Multa Plyer

P.S. Your kids also will learn to tell time without digital watches.

If this type of letter gets you an interview, and if you precall plan and practice for your interview, you will at least be asked to submit a resume. Resumes after interviews are more persuasive, since they 1) are completely customized for the buyer/hirer and 2) reinforce the positive impression made in the interview. This teaching position post-interview resume will contain the following:

"Job Objective: to teach fourth and fifth graders to love math and to add, subtract, divide, and multiply with confidence."

Your job objective must be the hiring person's job objective. Your resume must show how you will fit perfectly into their organization.

• XIX •

Don't Play
What's My Line?

What's My Line? was a once popular television show that featured guests who had unusual lines of work. The guest stayed hidden while the emcee gave a series of job clues to a celebrity panel. The panel was challenged to answer the show's theme question, "What's my line?"

Here are phrases from genuine, completed resumes. What's their line?

Resume #1

- "Development and execution of exchange-traded market strategies . . ."
- "Developed new risk management products including raw material inventory finance programs . . ."
- "Worked with overseas subsidiaries of US corporations to help them develop and implement risk management programs . . ."

Resume #2

- "Demonstrated capacity to innovate, restructure, and initiate."
- "Initiated worldwide Centers of Expertise."
- "Led corporate effort in creating Regional Business Direction Teams."
- "Created CTP's (core technology platforms) and appointed CTP leaders to leverage core technologies throughout the corporation."

- "Increased Records of Invention disclosures from fifty to one-hundred and fifty per year."

Resume #3

- "Project manager for the implementation of multisite MRP II system."
- "Reengineered US supply center locations."
- "Developed and implemented organizational infrastructure to support business plan."
- "Created direct divisional resources as well as leveraging existing operations and product development resources within a matrix management organization."

This kind of corporate-speak language is nonsensical. It doesn't inform, it obfuscates. And while such stilted business language is supposed to sound and read managerial, it is dumb. Anything that can be misunderstood will be misunderstood. Anything that is misunderstood reduces your chance of getting the job. Rather than "implemented organizational infrastructure to support business plan," write "hired and trained two product managers."

If your resume reads like a game-show quiz, you will stay behind the curtain for a long time. Write and speak in clear, plain, precise English. Read what you have written to a friend. If your friend cannot perfectly understand everything in your resume, rewrite it. Your resume should be crisp, clear, interesting, and memorable. Your resume should not have to carry the warning, "Do not operate heavy machinery after reading."

• XX •

The Job Interview
Is a Sales Call

*T*he hiring interview is a sales call. You are the product you want the customer to buy. You are also the salesperson responsible for selling the product. The customer is the hiring decision maker in the organization.

It is the decision maker's job, the interviewer's job, to decide if his or her organization should invest some of their resources and buy you. There are usually other important people in the hiring/purchase process. These other decision influencers—people who have some "yes" or "no" veto power on the hire—may include the interviewer's boss, her col-leagues, the president of the company. If any of the decision influencers are negative about buying you, your chances of making the sale are low. So, you must persuade everyone in the purchasing process that you are worth more than their investment in you.

Each decision influencer and decision maker has different needs and concerns. Your job is to deter-mine those needs and prove you can satisfy those needs. There is only one reason people hire some-one, and that reason is to solve a problem. You must uncover that problem, calculate the cost to the organization of not solving the problem, and demonstrate that you are the solution. There are six things you must do for every interview for every organization:

1. Precall plan each interview. Your precall is the plan you are going to follow during your interviews that will lead to a job. Before your visit, you review all your research on the

company. You consider how you are going to present your story. You make a plan.

2. Have at least one written objective to achieve in each interview. For example, one objective is to demonstrate a particular skill or definitive experience critical to your target company.

3. Conduct a preplanned, practiced needs analysis, asking careful, thoughtful questions. Write out the questions you intend to ask and practice asking them.

4. Listen intently and take notes. Customers like sellers who take notes.

5. Show something. You may have the chance to show examples of past work. You may show a survey you did on the company's customers.

6. Ask for a commitment. Plan how you intend to ask for the job or for further interviews.

The job interview is the most important part of the job-getting process. This is when you sell the employer on you. Do not treat the job interview casually. You cannot over-prepare. You cannot over-practice.

Your questions, your answers, your demeanor, your attitude will sell you. If you can persuade the hirer that you are the solution to their problem, you will get the job.

· XXI ·

Answer the Question, Why Should This Company Hire Me?

*I*f you don't know why a company should hire you, it is a good bet the company won't know either. You know yourself. You know your capabilities. After you have researched your target company, you are going to gain an understanding of how you can help the company, in the short term or longer term or both. How you can help is how you can sell yourself to the company.

Think as if you worked for the target company. What would you expect from someone with your skills? Your answer as to why the company should hire you has to in some way involve the economics of the company. Your answer, for example, might be one of the following.

The company should hire me because:

I can sell more of their products.

I can help collect overdue accounts.

I can better train the truck drivers, thereby reducing accidents and late deliveries.

I can negotiate lower interest rates with the banks.

I can conceptualize and introduce new products.

I can reduce the costs of their telephone systems.

I can launch their products in China.

I can improve their product design.

I can reduce their product assembly time.

I can improve their advertising to generate more sales leads.

I can navigate government bureaucracies and speed up product approvals.

Ultimately you will be hired, and ultimately your success will depend on how well you help the organization prosper. Prosperity depends on having customers. It is everyone's job in the company to help the company get and keep customers. If you can demonstrate how you will get and keep customers, any good company will hire you.

· XXII ·

Always Have a
Sales Call / Job Interview Objective

*E*very good salesperson prepares a written objective before making a sales call. Good selling objectives, for example, include meeting all the decision makers, demonstrating the product and getting a product specified on a blueprint, and getting a purchase order. So too must every job seeker have a written objective for every interview. Your interview objective is precisely like a sales call objective. Knowing what you wish to achieve in every interview helps you shape your job-getting strategy and design your interview questions.

Good interview objectives include the following:

- To get the job
- To learn about other possible job opportunities
- To get invited to return for more interviews
- To get past any screeners to meet the real decision maker(s)
- To get an offer to work on a trial basis as an independent contractor (for, say, six to ten weeks)
- To get a consulting project
- To get a referral to another good company

At some point in your meetings with your target customer, it is not only appropriate but imperative that you present your objective and ask to make the objective happen. For example: "Mr. Fitzhugh, based on my research and based on what was discussed in some of my interviews, it appears that your company is interested in how you benchmark in R & D innovation among your competitors. This issue is more a project than a full-time job. I am willing to take on the benchmarking task as a consulting project. That way we could learn more about each other, and you will get some valuable information. Why don't we give it a try?" Then wait until Mr. Fitzhugh answers.

Mr. Fitzhugh may hire you for the full-time job. Or he may hire you for the consulting project, which could lead to the full-time job. Or Mr. Fitzhugh could continue to demur. If so, Mr. Fitzhugh will most likely state his reason for not hiring you. This will be an objection you may or may not be able to overcome, but at least you now will know what the customer really wants.

· XXIII ·

Precall Plan
Every Job Interview

*B*ecause a job interview is a sales call where you are the salesperson selling yourself, the meeting must be preplanned. All great salespeople plan every sales call. So must you. Ninety percent of all sales calls are won or lost in precall. You must precall every interview—every person—you are going to see at the target company. If your interview schedule has five meetings, you will need five precall plans. If you are asked back for follow-up interviews, those too must be preplanned.

In addition to the background homework and

research you must conduct before contacting the company—and certainly before visiting the company—you should invest at least five to fifteen hours in precall planning for your first interview. Precall planning is done in writing. It is not done in your head or while jogging or in the shower. Precall planning is not done on the way to the interview. It is done with a pad and pencil or mouse and keyboard or hammer and chisel. Start your precall planning with your answer to the question, "Why should this company hire me?" The answer is the basis for why it makes economic sense for the company to hire you. The answer is your value proposition to your customer, the company. To effectively answer this question you must do as much pre-interview homework as possible, and you must listen with care to the answers to your interview questions.

Be absolutely sure you know how to pronounce everybody's name. America is a stew of new and old ethnicities. There are many difficult names to manage, but pronouncing someone's name correctly is a sign of respect. Correct name pronunciation, especially in a first meeting, delights the customer and instantly gives you a positive edge. If you were interviewing Sam Hamam or Umesh Cooduvalli or Beverly Ng, how much precall practice would you require? Think through exactly what next-step commitment you need from the hiring person that will lead to your job. This commitment is your job interview objective.

Craft and write out the needs analysis questions you intend to ask during each interview. Practice asking the questions. It is appropriate to refer to your written list of questions during your interviews. Do not take notes when the interviewer is asking you questions, which usually occurs at the beginning of the interview. Such note taking may make people uneasy. You can take notes as the interviewer answers your questions. Do take careful notes of the interviewers' answers. Taking notes is always appropriate. But you are not taking notes in History 101. You are only capturing what you will later review or use in follow-up communications. Maintain some eye contact. Stay in the discussion.

And please, please, please don't pull out a laptop and start key pounding (use the laptop later, after you get the job).

Anticipate being asked questions related to your experience, to your qualifications, personal goals, personal interests, and the underlying reasons for your interest in the company. Most interviewers will have concerns—your age, your ability, your health, your character, your work history, or your background. Interviewers will ask you directly about some issues, but not about others. If concerns exist, you must handle them in order to get hired. Properly handling these concerns starts with anticipation and starts in precall. Plan and practice how you intend to ask for the job or for a commitment to an action that will directly lead to getting the job.

Hiring companies like candidates who have done their homework and prepared for interviews. They infer that good work to get a job signals good work on the job.

· XXIV ·

Job Interview
Precall Planner

*T*his is an example of a precall planner you may use to prepare for every interview and every interviewer. You may adapt or modify this form if it is not suited to your situation; however, you must use some formal planning device. Expect, at times, to be interviewed by two or three people at the same time. You must precall for each interviewer. Don't be discouraged if you can't always complete the planner. The more you learn about the interviewers at your target customer, and the more experience you get in precall planning, the easier and more effective your planning will be. Every interviewer. Every interview. No exceptions.

Precall Planner Worksheet

1. **Organization name**_____
   Phonetic pronunciation*_____

2. **Interview Schedule**
   A. Interview with _____
   Location _____ **Time** _____

   B. Interview with _____
   Location _____ **Time** _____

   C. Interview with _____
   Location _____ **Time** _____

3. **Snapshot summary of organization**
   Industry_____
   Products_____
   Customers_____

Competitors_____
Reputation and image_____
News tidbits_____

4. Why this company should hire you (what
   dollarizable value you will bring, what
   problem you will solve).

_____

_____

_____

_____

The Interview
1. Interviewer's name_____
   Phonetic pronunciation*_____
   Title and responsibilities_____
   Role and influence in the hiring
   decision**_____

Interviewer profile: background, reporting relationship, likes, dislikes_____

_____

2. Interview (sales call) objective_____

_____

3. Needs analysis question to ask (note: these questions can be organized on separate pages, as you will have numerous questions).

- _____
- _____
- _____
- _____
- _____

4. Possible interviewer concerns

- _____
- _____
- _____
- _____

5. **Preplanned, practiced answers to concerns**

- _____
- _____
- _____
- _____

6. **Getting a commitment to your interview objective. Write exactly how you intend to ask the hirer (customer) for the commitment you desire.**

_____

_____

_____

7. **Follow up**
   Action_____
   Due date_____

* Particularly relevant for difficult to pronounce names and for foreign companies

**You must determine how the hiring decision is made, who is involved, and the relative influence of each person involved in the hiring process.

• XXV •

No One Cares What You Like

No one cares how you want to use your experience. No one cares that you like working with people. No one cares that at this stage of your career you do or don't want to do such and such. No one cares that you love to write. The only thing the hiring people care about is their problem. If hiring you can help solve their problem, then you have a shot at the job. If the hiring people don't think you can help, it doesn't matter what your background contains; you won't get the job. When interviewing for a job, don't say, "What I really like to do is marketing," or "What gets me going is to solve problems." Don't say, "What appeals to me is the opportunity to use my creativity, my education, my experience." No one cares!

Your objective in the interview is to find out what the hiring people, the customers, like. You must uncover what they need, what they are looking for, and why. Find out that the company needs a meeting planner who can eliminate airline and hotel reservation errors, thereby reducing costs. Now your love of managing complicated projects is relevant. But don't tell the interviewer "I like to administer complex projects." Rather, ask the interviewer, "So, is it correct that you are looking for someone who pays attention to details and is well organized?" If the customer responds positively, then you ask, "Would you be interested in hearing how my experience managing the graduation exercises at the college where I once worked fits your job requirements?" Then show how your experience fills their need. It doesn't matter what you like. It matters what the hirers like and if they like you. If they like your experience and they like you, you will get the job.

· XXVI ·

Great First Interview Questions

*B*ecause the job interview is a sales call it should be planned, practiced, and conducted as a sales call. One of the most critical factors in making a sale is doing a needs analysis. A needs analysis is when you ask questions to find out precisely what the customer wants so as to best position those features and benefits of your product (yourself) that satisfy the customer's needs. You must diagnose before you prescribe. Interviewers like candidates who ask thoughtful questions. They like candidates who are truly interested in the company. Asking questions—

and listening to the answers—is a point of difference. Most if not all of the other candidates will be talking about themselves. Interviewers will believe you are really smart if you ask these smart questions.

Note: You may know the answers to many of these questions based on your homework. If the interviewer's response is wrong, don't correct him. If the interviewer's response surprises you or offends you or is off base, don't react. Make a note. If you don't understand an answer, ask for further explanation.

1. Why is your company successful?
2. What must your company do to stay successful?
3. How does your company make money?
4. What are your strategies to get and keep customers?
5. What is the vision for this company in three years?
6. What does it take to succeed here?

7. Why have other people failed here?

8. What were the reasons you went to work here?

9. Are your competitors ABC, Inc., and XYZ, Inc.?

10. What differentiates your products and company from the competitors?

11. Why are (the target job position, e.g., salespeople or scientists or accountants) important to your company?

12. How important are (target job position:___) to the company?

13. What are your expectations for the job?

14. What important (job position task:___) is not being done well today?

15. What are you looking for?

16. What kind of training is available?

17. What is your hiring process?

18. Who else is involved in the decision to hire?

19. What are the concerns about this position?

20. What will it take for someone like myself to get accepted by your company?

21. Is there any question I should be asking that I'm not asking?

A good question is one that when answered teaches both the questioner and the responder something. A good question signals to the customer, the hirer, good things about you.

· XXVII ·

Don't Talk
in an Interview

A hiring interview is a sales call. Don't talk or tell. Answer, ask, listen, and sell. You are the salesperson, you are the product, and your customer is the interviewer. Because the job interview is a sales call it must be planned, practiced, and conducted as a sales call. Every sales call must have a written objective. Your objective on your first interview is to get a second interview or extend the first interview past what was planned, or both. The most successful salespeople understand that during a sales call the customer should be talking 80 percent of the time, and the salesperson should be listening 80 percent of the time. The successful salesperson allocates his or her 20 percent of "talking time" to answer the interviewers' questions, and to ask questions.

On the first interview you must conduct a needs analysis. A needs analysis is when you ask questions to find out what the customer needs and wants. A proper needs analysis gets the customer—the hirer—talking and allows you to take notes. Your questions must be crafted before the interview. They must be based on homework.

When the interviewer asks you a question, answer the question and stop talking. You should try to anticipate possible interviewer questions in your precall planning before the interview. (Precall planning is the time spent preparing for your sales call, your interview). You must answer the question directly, honestly, briefly, and fully. Because you may have anticipated the question, your answer should highlight your skills and good qualities. When you have answered the question precisely, stop talking. Do not embellish, stray from the point, or volunteer new information. Be quiet. Wait for the interviewer to finish the line of inquiry. If the interviewer is finished, it may be appropriate for you to ask one of your pre-planned needs-analysis questions. If you do ask one of your questions, be quiet after asking, and let the customer answer. Intelligent questions are rare. Asking intelligent questions signals intelligence. Intelligence is a quality good companies want. Compelling questions cause good answers, elevating the content of the interview. Good interviews elevate the interviewer, the hirer. When you ask a good question, let the interviewer answer, and let the interviewer answer fully. Don't say something while the interviewer is thinking. Don't retract the question because she has not responded quickly enough for you. If the customer understands your question, then to speak before she does is an interruption. Unless she nods off and falls on the floor after you ask a question, be quiet and listen.

Asking thoughtful questions is a point of difference, and will separate you from the other talk, talk, talk candidates.

Douglas MacArthur, the legendary World War II army general, was looking to hire a new aide. After a staff review of candidates, MacArthur interviewed the "short list." One of the potential aides was a young lieutenant. At the beginning of the interview the general asked the lieutenant, "Did you have any trouble finding the place?" "No, sir," answered the lieutenant, who then asked, "Sir, what is your view of the role of the army in winning the war here in the Pacific?" For one hour, interrupted only by the lieutenant's occasional "uh-huh," and "Could you elaborate?" the great general talked.

At the end of the "interview," the lieutenant was offered the job. Later, Douglas MacArthur told one of his colonels that the young lieutenant was one of the most intelligent officers he had met, and asked great questions. The lieutenant was a sell guy, not a tell guy. So you should be.

• XXVIII •

Handling
Interviewer Concerns

*B*ecause the economic and personal costs of a mis-hire are so high, hirers are cautious. They will always be concerned that they are making the correct hiring decision. Hirers may worry about the candidate's work ethic, experience level, enthusiasm, smarts, integrity, people skills, sexual orientation, age, gender, marital situation, background, competency, ability to get the job done, and morals. These worries may be trivial, unwarranted, illegal, important or unimportant. But they are always real—and for various reasons, these issues may be hidden concerns.

You must uncover as many hidden concerns as possible. You must provide some type of assurance to allay the interviewer's concerns. Handling the company's concerns starts in pre-interview planning, by anticipating any objections to hiring you. Once you determine possible objections, you can begin to develop strategies to handle the objections.

For example, some job seekers may believe the following situations could be barriers to getting hired:

- At 50 years of age, too old
- At 21 years of age, no experience
- 6 jobs in 10 years, job hopper

It is easier to handle a hirer's concern if he or she voices the concern; however, there are discrimination laws that prevent people from asking certain questions. Interviewers will try to get to their issues in indirect ways. Code phrases are used to get answers to questions that may be prohibited to ask by law or convention. In a phone screening interview, a hirer might ask, "What are the ages of your children?" This is a clue that the hirer is concerned about age. An interviewer might ask, "What values did your parents try to instill in you?" This is a code phrase designed to learn about your background, and what are, or were, your parents' occupations. If the interviewer asks, "Is there anything that might prevent you from, say, going on a trip for two weeks?" the interviewer may be concerned about your health, your marital situation (single parent), or your work ethic. It is the burden of the candidate to listen carefully for any question that is an interviewer's code phrase for approaching an area of concern. At such point, the candidate must answer the question with a preplanned response that satisfies the hirer's possible objection.

For example, the candidate who thinks that being fifty-five may be a problem is asked, "How do you go about making decisions?" This question, or any question that provides a segue into a preplanned response is the candidate's cue. The prepared candidate who has anticipated that his age may be a concern answers as follows: "My decision-making approach has been developed over years of hands-on experience working with all kinds of people, on all kinds of problems, with varying amounts of facts and data. Today I know a lot more that I did even ten years ago about listening to other people, sifting fact from fiction, and then deciding. It took me—and I dare say it takes others—lots of battles to make seasoned, reasoned, sound decisions. Does that answer your question, and are there other areas of my extensive experience that you may want to ask about?"

Ronald Reagan, then in his late sixties, was running against a much younger Walter Mondale for president of the US. Mr. Reagan knew that the public had some concerns about his age. In a masterful stroke, on a nationally televised debate, Mr. Reagan stole the issue by saying, "I promise not to make my opponent's youth and inexperience an issue in this campaign." Clearly preplanned and practiced, this humorous rejoinder deflated a potentially thorny issue. Mondale said in a subsequent interview that he was convinced that he had lost the election then and there. Conversely, Ronald Reagan won the job then and there. Precall planning and practice closed the sale.

Knowing the answer to the question, Why should the company hire you? gives you a bedrock position to make your case. If you know how the company will benefit from hiring you, then with planning and creativity, any hiring concern can be handled.

• XXIX •

Show Something on Every Interview

Great salespeople show something on every sales call. They may show a sample product, examples of relevant work, case histories, and research summaries. But they always show something. According to certain studies, salespeople who show something have a 65 percent greater chance of making the sale than those who show nothing. Because the job interview is a sales call, you will increase the probability of getting the job if you show something.

You will have done exhaustive research on the company before your interview. You will have read all available information, tried the products, talked to people who know the company. You will have answered the question, Why should this company hire me? You will have ideas on how the company can increase sales, reduce waste, outsmart the competition, and tap into new markets. This pre-interview homework can always be packaged into an effective showpiece.

For examples, you may show the interviewer:

- A survey of what the interviewer's company's customers are thinking.
- A research report on the competition.
- New product ideas.
- Product packaging improvements.
- A summary of market trends.

Good people in good companies will be flattered that you invested your time unselfishly in an effort to help. They will see you as inventive, as a self-starter, as someone unafraid to express ideas. No other job candidate will do this.

Consequently, your creative approach will be a point of difference (a point of difference is something about a product that is different or unique. A point of difference is something memorable that will distinguish you from other job seekers). What you show can be a lead-in to some of your preplanned questions. If you are showing a comparison of the product literature of the companies in the interviewer's industry you can ask about market shares, competitive strategy, relative growth rates. If you are showing a mock-up of a new dispenser you can ask about research and development (R&D) investments, attitudes toward innovation, customer preferences. If you are showing a set of photographs of storefronts and store windows you can ask about merchandising, distribution, and retail strategies.

Show up early. Show yourself. And show something that benefits the customer, your target company, thereby benefiting you. Show something inventive and on target and the show's over. You've got the job!

• XXX •

Ask to Do
a Demonstration

Neither the company nor the employee knows how the job will work out until after the person has worked at the company for several weeks. The company might be disappointed, and so too might the employee. A win-win arrangement is to work for an interested, almost-sold company as an independent contractor for a reasonable period of time. Another get-to-know-you solution is to work on a consulting project for the hiring company. Both these routes are a way for you to demonstrate your worth.

Any buying decision at an organization carries some risk. One risk is that the product will not perform as claimed. If the product does not perform as expected, the organization usually experiences some kind of economic loss such as a reduction in competitiveness, a missed opportunity, less gross margin, or less net profit. But companies don't buy: People in the company buy. Because individuals make the purchase decision, there is another risk when the product does not perform as expected. That risk is the risk of colleague criticism. If the colleague criticism is effective (which may or may not reflect the truth) the purchase decision maker could experience loss of status, loss of colleague confidence, loss of promotability, or loss of job.

Consequently, businesses and organizations prefer to test any product before they buy it. They want to be sure the product will perform as claimed. They want to reduce the risk of making an unworthy investment. If they can't test the product they use other ways to get proof that they are not making a mistake. They review the experience of other users.

They visit the selling company's plants and facilities. They ask for references. They ask for some kind of product demonstration. Sometimes companies are so economically desperate for the solution the product promises that they buy and hope for good results—and sometimes, when buying a new product from a new company, they trust their expertise, they trust their instincts, and they trust the new company's salesperson.

All of this is true for the hiring decision, the decision to buy—to invest—in someone. Companies do not want to make hiring mistakes. Hiring mistakes carry significant costs. These costs vary by the importance of the job, but they are always real. Some experts estimate the total cost of a mis-hire to be two to four times a person's salary. Economic costs associated with a mis-hire could include fees to recruitment firms, severance payments, legal fees, insurance coverage, opportunity loss (e.g., an uncovered sales territory), recruitment costs, advertising, retraining, wasted management time, and termination costs. The people doing the hiring in organizations try to avoid hiring mistakes by using recruiters, search firms, personality tests, background checks, reference checks, and extensive interviews of candidates (all of which are real hiring costs). Many organizations hope their tests and interviews simulate how the candidate will perform in their workplace. For example, professional athletic teams have tryouts, where prospective new hires (players) run timed sprints, scrimmage with other proven players, pitch to hitters, undergo personality tests. Some companies ask interviewees to respond to hypothetical life situations or answer riddles so they can evaluate candidates' ability to handle stress, or handle whatever the company thinks its tests are designed to uncover. But the true test is to evaluate the person in action, on the job.

If the hirer isn't making the hiring decision in a reasonable and timely manner, it may be appropriate to propose a demonstration. Ask the hirer, "If there were a low-risk way for you to evaluate me in your workplace, would you consider it?" If the answer is yes or maybe, tell the customer you are willing to work on a trial basis. You will be an escapable expense. Ask, "Let me give you a demonstration of the value I can deliver, OK?" When you get an agreement, go to the plate and hit one downtown.

Would you buy a pair of expensive shoes without first trying them on? Would you buy perfume without first smelling it? Why should a company hire you without proof of your worth? A successful demonstration is worth a thousand resumes.

· XXXI ·

Don't Order
Linguini with Marinara Sauce

You may be interviewed over lunch or dinner. Some companies deliberately interview candidates in a restaurant setting to observe how the job seeker might act with customers. Some hirers are interested in the candidate's manners, poise, dialogue skills, and social skills. Whatever the hirer's purpose, yours is not to eat lunch.

In precall planning for your interview, you will have created a written sales-call objective for the restaurant meeting. Achieving your written objective is your purpose at the meeting. You are not at lunch to eat or drink. You are there to get the job.

Don't order anything that will splash or stain. Don't order anything you have to spin, swirl, or spoon. Don't order anything you have to touch or eat with your fingers. Use your fingers to hold your pen to take notes during the conversation. Don't talk with food in your mouth. In asking your pre-planned questions and responding to the inter-viewer's comments you may not have time to eat anything. That's OK. Cut your food into very small pieces so your plate doesn't appear untouched.

Don't order alcohol. If you are at a place where wine is automatically served, say in France or Napa Valley, say thank you and leave the glass full (unless you are seeking a job as a wine taster).

Don't let all the tableware and glassware faze you. The only glass you need use is the one filled with water. Use the shortest fork first. Read a book on table manners. That's it.

Even if it's an Italian restaurant, do not order linguini with marinara or tomato sauce. A young woman was spending a full day interviewing with a biopharmaceutical company, seeking a job as a product manager. She was experienced and professional. She wore pearls, an ivory-colored silk blouse, and a tailored skirt. Part of the interviewing schedule included lunch with three potential colleagues. At lunch, one of the interviewers raved about the pasta vongole and ordered it. So too did the job candidate. She promptly speckled her blouse rosso Siciliano. The sauce stains were obvious. One interviewer was thinking, "Oh my. That blouse must have cost her a hundred dollars." Another thought, "I never should have recommended the linguini." The third interviewer said to herself, "Now what?"

The job seeker lost her poise. Her confidence was shattered. For the rest of the day she self-consciously tried to hide and minimize the damage. Her focus bounced between her blouse and her interviewers. She blew the sales call. But she did not blow the sale. She was lucky. Her last interview of the day, with the company CEO, was rescheduled for an early breakfast the next day. The next morning the intrepid job seeker wore pearls. She wore silk. She ordered grapefruit juice—not tomato!—and scrambled eggs. She sipped the juice. She asked questions and took notes. She never touched her fork. She got the job.

Learn this lesson in this book, not in La Trattoria or Ristorante Italia.

· XXXII ·

Look Like a Ballplayer

*I*t was a ragtag high-school team; some kids had their shirts hanging out of their pants. Some kids had their socks on wrong. Others wore gold chains. Hats were backwards. They looked sloppy and they played sloppily. The players missed signals, made errors, threw to the wrong base, showed up late for practice, and horsed around in the dugout. They lost games they should have won.

The new coach's first practice started in the locker room. He admonished the team: "If you can't act like a ballplayer, at least look like a ballplayer!" The coach showed the boys how to roll their stirrup socks into their uniform pants. He showed them the proper way to buckle and button. The brims of the caps were rounded alike. Earrings and necklaces and watches went into the lockers. The new coach taught the players how to stand for the national anthem, how to dress for road games, and how to run on and off the field.

Coincidentally, on-field physical and mental errors dramatically dropped. The team won a lot of games. The kids may not have made it to the major leagues, but they learned major-league attitude. When you show up for your interview, look like a ballplayer. Be cool, clean, confident. Shoes shined. No dandruff. Perfect lipstick. Neat notebook. Organized precall paperwork.

Appearance isn't everything, clothes don't make the woman, beauty is only skin deep, you can't tell a book by its cover, there's more than meets the eye—and every other cliché in the book. But proper appearance is something. It shows self-respect, respect for the hirer, attention to detail. Appearance is an important part of the packaging of your product, and the product is you.

· XXXIII ·

Make Them
Feel Good

*T*here are only two reasons people buy things: to feel good or to solve a problem. There are no other reasons. If the product makes the person feel good and solves the problem, then the chances for the sale are high. This is also true of the hiring process. Hiring people look first to solve a problem—to fill a company, business, or organization need. Not always, but usually, the hiring person must feel good about their purchase—their hire. In fact, experienced management recruiters believe that "good chemistry" between the hiring persons and the candidate is at least 80 percent, if not more, of the hiring equation. So you must make the hirers feel good about you. If you demonstrate you have the ability or potential to solve the organization's hiring need, and if you make the hiring people feel good about you, then you will be hired.

Here is what makes hiring people feel good about hiring someone.

The candidate:

- Will fit in with the other employees well enough to neither be destructive nor self-destruct.
- Is technically competent or trainable.
- Answers questions directly, honestly, and concisely.
- Is affordable; is within the means of the organization.
- Shows genuine interest in the company and the job.
- Demonstrates having done homework on the company, and is knowledgeable about the issues facing the company.

- Values the purpose of the company, and therefore values the purpose of the job.
- Is nice, well mannered, likable.
- Has enthusiasm, pep, energy. Laughs.
- Is smart enough.
- Has an "I can do it. I can get it done. I will do it. No problem" attitude.
- Asks positively phrased questions that cause the interviewer to think, and which engage the interviewer.
- Takes notes.
- Does not invade other people's physical or social space.
- Sends a thank-you note to each interviewer.

There is a difference between being friends and being friendly. You are not expected to be a friend. Being friendly is better. Being friendly makes people feel good. Be friendly.

• XXXIV •

Flatter and Wow Them with Your Interest

A prestigious liberal arts college was conducting an international search for a new president. The challenges the new president would face were unlike any in the country. The issues were not just the typical fund-raising and faculty bickering. This college had to change its neighborhood environment, rebuild its physical infrastructure, elevate its fine reputation even higher, and build a first-rate administration. But none of this was outlined in the recruiting information, not specified in the "job description." The college trustees received over two hundred applications, most highly qualified and motivated. A few applicants persisted past the resume stage, sending a follow-up letter or making a call. Most of the candidates depended on the brilliance of their resumes to get them on the short list of people to be invited for an interview.

Only one candidate made it impossible for the trustees to exclude him from the short list. This candidate wrote to trustees, had powerful friends call trustees, and asked outright to be considered. Although he did not fit the original profile, the trustees were impressed with the candidate's vigor and invited him to participate in a preordained series of interviews designed to cull and choose.

Unlike other candidates, who puffed with their record and accomplishments and degrees, who asked for directions to the college, who mispronounced the chairman of the board of trustees' name, or expected a limousine pickup, the dark horse stunned and delighted the trustees. The unlikely candidate knew the college's history (better than several trustees did). He had toured the neighborhood, visited merchants and tavern owners, talked to alumni, researched the town and the state's political apparatus. He asked homework based, thoughtful questions that zeroed in on the institution's biggest problems. He didn't let the trustees interpret his background and experience. Instead, he offered ideas and solution approaches, with a dollop of past successes as credibility. The trustees were flattered that someone cared so much about the college they shepherded.

Everybody has pluses and minuses. But if the seller—the candidate—can convince the customer—the hiring people—that his or her pluses outweigh the minuses, the chances of the sale—the hire—go up. When all has been asked and all has been said, and all candidates reviewed, if one person asked for the job, that act alone is often decisive. This candidate said to the trustees, face to face, "I understand your vision. I believe in your vision. I am not here to fail. I can make your vision happen. May I do this for you?"

The trustees agreed that if the candidate's on-the-job energy and persistence were as good as his job-getting approach, he was worth the risk.

• XXXV •

How to Play
Parlor Games

S ome companies give candidates stress interviews. Two or three interviewers gang up on the
candidate, asking trick questions supposedly geared
to test ability to act under pressure, to gauge intelligence, to judge emotional response. For example,
you may be asked,

> "There are three seconds left in a basket-
> ball game. Your team is down two points. You
> have the ball. With slightly lower odds of

making a three-point shot to win versus a two-pointer to tie, which shot should you take. Quick! What would you do?"

Or,

"Why are manhole covers round? Give us two reasons."

These interviews are stupid. The questions are parlor games masquerading as insightful management—but if you want to work for such a company, here's what to do:

First pause and think before you answer any question, even if you know the answer. When interviewing, a second of silence can seem like an hour to the interviewee. This is not the case for the interviewer. In fact a five- or ten-second pause before an answer will show that you care about the quality of your answer. You are not being graded on response time.

Follow these tips:

1. As part of your pre-interview homework, try to talk to other people who interviewed with the company. They will tell you about any trick questions. Forewarned is fore-armed.

2. If you do learn about any such questions, pre-call plan your responses, and practice how you will deliver your response.

3. Don't be surprised by any ambush interviews. Always assume that there will be some surprises. When you encounter a stress question, ask the interviewer, "Are there rules on how to answer that question?" This will give you time to think.

4. Also ask, "What is the purpose of that question?"

5. If asked what you would do in a certain situation, ask, "If that scenario you described is typical, wouldn't the response already have

been developed in some kind of in-house crisis-planning session?"

6. Ask, as part of your answer, "If I worked for *(name of company)*, would I be expected to decide on a similar action without permission, coaching, or management involvement?"

7. Ask, "Am I supposed to answer that question as someone who has been well trained, well coached, and empowered, or someone who has not been well coached?"

There are usually no correct answers to parlor-game questions. How you respond is as important as your response. For some hirers stress interviews are like hazing, a little hurdle to join the club. Play their games by your rules. That's how to win.

• XXXVI •

Always Ask for the Order

*A*t some point in the interviewing process, you must ask for the job if you want to be hired. Asking to be hired is equivalent to a salesperson asking for the order, asking to close the sale. Asking for the order is one of the most important factors for sales success, yet it is estimated that 95 percent of all salespeople never ask for the order. Consequently, the simple act of asking for the order, asking to be hired, is itself a point of difference.

Put the crucial importance of asking for the job in context: If you are trying for a job and there are nine other candidates, not one of the other nine will ask for the job! "Ask and ye shall receive," sayeth the Good Book. Heed the Russian proverb, "To ask is no sin, to be refused is no calamity." By asking for the job, you increase your odds of being hired by your target company by more that 50 percent.

Asking for the order is not necessarily easy. It is a difficult act for many people; however, it is a critical job-getting requirement. Be aware of the reasons why people don't ask for the job. If you know the reasons you can guard against them. You can avoid kidding yourself with some socially acceptable rationalization for not asking. If you know the reasons why people don't ask for the order, you can face the reasons squarely. You can plan an asking, or closing, approach and then do it.

Here are some of the reasons people don't ask for the order:

- Fear of rejection. People don't like rejection. People especially don't like it when, as in being rejected for a job, the rejection feels intensely personal.

- Believe asking is beneath them. Some people believe that asking for the sale is undignified or that what they are selling is so obviously the answer that there is no need to ask.
- Believe asking is impertinent. These people think that asking a question puts the other person on the spot, and makes them feel uncomfortable. But that is only true if you ask an embarrassing question.
- Don't know how to ask. Asking questions means asking, not telling. And it means waiting for the other person to answer. Too many people talk over their own questions.
- Think they don't have to ask. Some people believe they already know the answers, whether they do or not.

Despite the reasons, you must ask the hirer for the job. It may be your only chance. What do you have to lose? If the hirer is favorably impressed, your question may help the buyer favorably decide. If the hirer doesn't like you, you aren't getting the job anyway. If the customer, the hirer, is neutral— weighing your case against others—and you ask and the other candidate does not, you will get the nod.

Asking for the job can be done directly, but an indirect approach also works. For example, you might end the interview by summing up your understanding of the job, and then saying, "Based on my understanding of the job requirements, I am confident I can do what you want. What do you think?"

Or you might say, "I understand that experience in the industry is important to you and I don't have such direct experience, but I have a proven record of learning other industries quickly. I have successfully managed salespeople for five years. And I know how to sell to your customers. Do you think that these other skills outweigh the one issue, and make me an acceptable candidate?"

In your follow-up letter, sent one day after the

interview, you will restate your case and add that you doubt the company will find a more interested or dedicated candidate. Close your letter with a benefit you will bring to the company. For example, "If Steelton Corp. wants to dramatically improve customer service, I can make that happen. Thank you."

Know this: Buyers expect to be asked and want to be asked. How you comport yourself in the hiring process signals to the hirer how you will act on the job. If you ask for the order before you are working, then you will ask for the order while working. Companies want people who ask for the order. Listen and learn from John Fogarty's great song "Centerfield" when he sings, "Put me in, Coach. I'm ready to play. Today!"

• XXXVII •

Always Send a Thank-you Note

*F*ill the postman's sack with thank-you letters. Send notes to everyone you meet, send them often, send them early. Show your manners, respect, potential, and class.

Networking is one avenue that people use to find jobs. Job seekers meet people who may have a job opening, know of possible job opportunities, or who have influence, contacts, and referrals. It is almost always true that the people who have the most influence or contacts are the most difficult to meet. These people are busy. Their meeting with a job seeker is a generous investment of time. It is astonishing how often this investment in the job seeker does not even rate a thank-you note.

The head of a communications company in Chicago has graciously met with job seekers over one hundred times. He figures that he has heard from only 10 percent of the job seekers that he has tried to help. What amazes this executive is that he often does not hear from someone whose new job was a direct result of his efforts. The reason he still bothers to help job seekers is because he once was in their place. But when his networking got him a job he sent a thank-you note.

Management recruiters (a.k.a. headhunters) often speak with dismay about their experiences with executives they place in important jobs. Even the desperate job seeker who gets a plum job via the recruiter's efforts often forgets who helped him.

People in the network are in it because they have influence and reach that can be used in positive or damaging ways. People in the network value loyalty and courtesy, and they have excellent memories.

Don't Send a Resume

This is important to understand, because the business world is a small world. The business world is in constant motion. Companies get acquired. Competitors merge. Executives move from company to company. Your fierce competitor today can be your boss tomorrow. The person you worked with twenty years and two companies ago can emerge as the new leader of your organization. And people do lose jobs more than once. There are people in the job market today who are once again needful of the network. Who will get the help: the person who developed "assistance amnesia," or the grateful job seeker who took a few minutes to send a simple thank-you note?

Job-seeking events which merit a follow-up note are job interviews, network meetings, phone conversations, rejections, and job acceptances. Job acceptances require an informational thank-you note to everyone previously involved in the search. A remembrance today will be remembered tomorrow.

Get Five Points Every Day

*T*he four events that lead to landing a sale are the same events needed to land a job. The four specific events are 1) getting a lead, referral, or introduction to a potential hirer; 2) getting an appointment with the person making the hiring decision; 3) meeting the hiring person; and 4) getting a commitment from the decision maker to hire you, or a commitment to an action that directly leads to hiring you.

You must work every day to get contacts, appointments, interviews, and commitments. Assign each event a point value. A lead is worth one point. An appointment is two points. An interview is three points. And a commitment is four points. A good daily goal is five points, comprising any combination of point/event values.

The daily point system is a superb time and effort prioritization tool. It forces you to allocate and use your time on those activities that lead to a job. It reduces, if not eliminates, procrastination and feel-good "busy work." If you do get five points a day (or four or six or whatever is a reasonable stretch) you will have a calendar full of potential job-getting opportunities.

Try the point system for ten days. You may not get a job, but you will be much closer to a job than if you sent out five hundred resumes to a mailing list.

• XXXIX •

Keep a Daily Job-hunting To-do List

*F*or most hardworking, responsible, or ambitious people, not having a job is high stress. People worry. They question their self-worth. They sometimes find themselves not knowing what to do next. Whatever you feel, you must do something every day that leads you to getting a job. If you don't have a job you must do lots of things every day. If you have a job but are looking to change, you may not have as much time to search as you wish. But you also must do something every day until you get a new job. One key to maintaining your job-getting focus is a daily to-do list. You must have and complete a to-do list every single day until you get a job. Here are some of the activities that should be on your to-do list:

- Set a daily point goal.
- Review the newspapers in your target area (online, in library, or delivered).
- Use want-ads to get leads
- Review trade magazines that cover your target company's industry.
- Research to find a target company.
- Write an impact letter.
- Write a resu-letter.
- Write a boomerang letter.
- Send a thank-you note.
- Build a people database (a "people file").
- Add five names to your people file.
- Contact five people.
- Get a referral.

- Buy your target company's product.
- Visit a trade show for your target company's industry.
- Use on-line career opportunity sites to get leads.

· XL ·

The Job Seeker's Workday

5:30 A.M.	Rise, exercise, shower, and dress for work.
7:00 A.M.	Breakfast. Review all the help-wanted ads in all the papers serving your forty-mile radius target markets. Review all the Internet postings. Review "Who's Who" in *The Wall Street Journal* and all promotions in the business section of the newspapers.
8:30 A.M.	Write boomerang letters to all job openings that appear interesting.
9:30 A.M.	Identify one more target company. Use the *Standard Directory of International Advertisers*

and Advertising Agencies: The International Red Book, Dun and Bradstreet directories of business, and all sources.

10:30 A.M.	Develop your homework and research plan for one or more of your target companies.
11:00 A.M.	Continue homework and research on target companies.
2:00 P.M.	Write one impact letter.
3:00 P.M.	Precall plan your 5:30 interview.
5:20 P.M.	Arrive at your 5:30 interview.
6:15 P.M.	Write interview follow-up note.
6:30 P.M.	Spend time with your family. Or make risotto for yourself.
7:30 P.M.	Continue research on target companies.
9:15 P.M.	Plan next day.

• XLI •

Never Panic

When you do not have a job, it is OK to be concerned, but it is not OK to panic. This is especially important as time goes on and the job hunt seems hopeless. No matter how desperate you are, you must never show desperation to a potential hirer. You must beam confidence and control. Buyers are put off by salespeople who are desperate, uneasy, frightened. Confident salespeople comfort buyers. Generals reject fear-frozen soldiers—and fear-frozen soldiers don't become generals.

Here are ten tips to ward off panic, to defeat desperation, and to keep hope:

1. Dress each day as if you were at work. Dress and groom with care.
2. Keep to a rigid daily job-hunting work schedule.
3. Believe that each day of life is a gift.
4. There are worse situations than not having a job, such as disease. Be thankful.
5. Some very tough people tell themselves every day to "be brave." Do it.
6. Exercise vigorously every day.
7. The numbers are in your favor. The job market is huge. There is an organization that needs you.
8. You weren't personally rejected. Your timing did not match the organization's timing. Don't take rejection personally.
9. People who regularly have to make high-cost, split-second decisions often counsel

themselves to "stay calm." If you feel yourself starting to lose it, command yourself to stay calm. It works.

10. Stay in touch with your higher power.

And remember the immortal words of Cool Hand Luke (played by Paul Newman in the classic movie of the same name) after he bluffed to win a high-stakes poker game: "Sometimes nothing can be a mighty cool hand."

· XLII ·

Don't Ask
for Directions

Companies hire people to solve problems, to prevent problems, to make issues go away, to reduce pressures, to improve financially, to free up talent to use their talents. Companies hire people to take things off their collective to-do list. They do not want employees who add problems, bring unwanted baggage, who require unnecessary maintenance.

Employers want people who hit the road running; who are resourceful, self-reliant, able. During the hiring process, particularly for the first interview, heed the following:

Don't Send a Resume

- Don't ask for directions. If your customer (the hiring person) volunteers to fax directions, that's fine. Otherwise, find your way yourself and get there early. Don't put even the smallest item on your target customer's to-do list.
- Don't treat the receptionist, or anyone, as beneath you, as an inferior, as someone who works for you.
- Don't make demands. If you are negotiating compensation, for example, present your expectations, but no demands.
- Don't disparage or be negative about any past superiors, colleagues, or organizations. Companies value discretion. Saying nothing is appropriate. Who knows? That rotten boss may be the hiring person's favorite college roommate.
- Don't complain. Don't talk about how you feel. Don't talk about what's ailing you. No one cares.
- Don't ask about benefits. If the company has benefits and they want to hire you, the company

will tell you. If the company does not have certain benefits and they want to hire you, the company will tell you.

- Don't ask about your title, the size of your office, any perquisites, or the work hours.
- Don't ask how much travel or overtime or weekend work is required.

Your objective is to get a job. Your approach is to focus on the hiring person's agenda, not on your agenda. If the hiring company's agenda is unsuitable to you, or the culture of the company is off-putting to you, or if anything about the company is a showstopper, then drop out of the running. You can determine negatives with homework, observation, good questions, and keen listening.

If you need directions to the company, how much direction will you need to do a tougher job? If you need directions, how will you *give* direction, manage, or lead?

Good organizations want people who know the way or who will find the way.

• XLIII •

"I" Is a Bad Word

"*I*" is a special word that in the job-getting process should be used sparingly, if at all. "I" should never appear on a resume. Minimize using "I" in your letters. Use "You" instead. (For example, instead of "I will send you . . ." write "You will receive . . . .") Overuse of "I" in your interviews can be disastrous. Hiring organizations and the hirers in the organizations care about *their* issues and challenges. They don't care about you. There is little more off-putting to a hirer than the "I, I, I" candidate.

Hirers are looking for self-confidence, not self-centeredness. Hirers are looking for team players, not prima donnas. Hirers want credit makers, not credit takers.

The best salespeople say "you" instead of "I." The Cornell School of Hotel and Restaurant Management found that waiters who say "you" instead of "I" earn 20 percent more in tips. As a job seeker, you must adopt the best practices of great salespeople. Great salespeople listen more than they talk. Listen to yourself. If you have it, break the habit of making yourself the focal point of every sentence.

Don't start an answer with, "I think" or "It's my opinion." Just say what you think, or what your opinion is. Don't say "what I would like to do." What you would like to do is irrelevant. It is what the hirer would like to do that matters.

Using "I" about yourself and your past is boring. Using "I" about the future can be exciting. Hirers don't want to hear "I did this" and "I did that." Hirers do want to hear "I can do it." Hirers do want to hear "I will do it."

Optometrists use "I." You use "you."

• XLIV •

"Wind Me Up at Harvard!"

*T*his is a story about getting a job.

It was a young man's goal to get accepted to the Harvard Business School. He did homework on Harvard's admission process. The candidate learned he was younger that the average age of first-year MBA students. His business board scores (grad school equivalent to the college boards) were OK, not great. Harvard had meager experience with prior graduates from his college. He knew no one who had gone to the Havard Business School. He was not from a foreign country, not a minority, not anything special. His family had no influence. His college counseling office had little influence at Harvard. He had little money.

Harvard sent one of their admission officers to the candidate's college on a quasi-recruiting public relations visit. The Harvard representative gave a presentation and answered questions. At the end of the session, as everyone was leaving, the prospective candidate, the college student, approached the Harvard P.R. representative. The student asked one question, "How does one get into the Harvard Business School?" The fellow looked at the student and said, "No one has asked that question before." He then proceeded to explain that the admissions people use a number of factors to reduce the pool, to eliminate candidates. For example, if the business board scores are too low, that might be a reason to reject. The key to admission was getting the selection committee to read the extensive essays that were part of the application. If the essays were compelling, the candidate had a chance.

The prospective candidate was determined to

break through the gaggle of thousands of applications and get the selection committee to read his essays.

At that time the Sheraton Hotel chain was running television commercials and print ads, all with the slogan, "Keyed-up executives unwind at the Sheraton." The commercials featured a harried and hurried businessman, in a trenchcoat and hat and carrying a briefcase, with a big key in his back. The businessman was wound up tight, only slowing down at the hotel.

The candidate went to a toy store. He bought a Ken doll. He put a hat and a coat on the doll. He made a tiny cardboard briefcase. He pasted his picture over Ken's face. He bought a windup toy with a key in back, broke off the key, and stuck it in Ken's back. He replicated the Sheraton's keyed-up executive.

His classmates told him not to do it. It's unconventional, risky. The college counseling office told him not to do it. It's cutesy, not serious. Everyone told him not to do it. So he stopped asking other people's opinion.

The college student put the doll in a shoebox and sent it to Harvard Business School's director of admissions. In the box he slipped a card with the phrase, "Wind me up at Harvard."

The candidate received a letter several days later, remarking on the doll and promising to read his essays.

And yes, the young man is now a graduate of the Harvard Business School.

Getting into a competitive school is similar to getting hired by a good company. There are many qualified candidates. You have to stand out, distinguish yourself. You have to think like the hiring company, understand the hiring company's ethos and ego, and know why the company should hire you. You have to do more than the other candidates. You have to show the target organization that you are their type of person. You have to show high interest in the company. And you must be bold and creative and unafraid to demonstrate that you are a special person.

"Boldness has genius, power and magic in it."
—Johann Wolfgang Von Goethe